THE BIRTH OF STATES

SUCCESSFUL AND FAILED SECESSIONS

A Comparative Analysis of South Sudan,

Somaliland and Western Sahara

First Edition

JACOB DUT CHOL RIAK

Africa
World Books
Pty Ltd

A Note from the Publisher

The publisher wishes to acknowledge and thank Dr Douglas H. Johnson for his invaluable help and support for Africa World Books and its mission of preserving and promoting African cultural and literary traditions and history. Dr Johnson and fellow historians have been instrumental in ensuring that African people remain connected to their past and their identity. Africa World Books is proud to carry on this mission.

© Jacob Dut Chol Riak, 2021

ISBN: 978-0-6451109-1-3

Cover design, typesetting and layout: Africa World Books
Cover image: Balasoiu / Freepik

"So no matter where it takes hold, government of people and by people sets a single standard for all who would hold power. You must respect the rights of minorities and participate with a spirit of tolerance and compromise; you must place the interests of your people and the legitimate workings of the political process above your party. Without these ingredients, elections alone do not make true democracy."

President Barack Obama,
Cairo, June 4, 2009

Contents

Dedication

To my late lovely mother Daruka Aluel aka Aguet Ajang Duot: your love for education and self-emancipation can never be forgotten! I wish you were around now to see the educational fruits of your son. Continue resting in eternal peace, Mom!

To my lovely wife, Rechoh Achol Dau, thank you for your enthusiasm for our family's success and education; it is an epitome of my triumph.

Abstract

THIS BOOK EXAMINES different domestic and international factors that lead to support for secessions. It questions why South Sudan's secession was successfully supported by Western great powers while Somaliland and Western Sahara were not supported. It uses realist theory and norms of sovereignty as an analytical conceptual framework for understanding the national interests of the Western great powers in supporting independence and conferring sovereignty. It argues that support for secessions and international recognition have more to do with the great powers' own interests, particularly, the U.S., rather than the fulfillment of the criteria of international law.

The analysis examines six competing arguments (hypotheses) such as: history of conflict; agreed framework and commitment of local population; compatible norms and internationalized ethnic politics; status of the mother state in the eyes of the international community; economic benefits, and security and stability interests in the case of South Sudan. A comparison of these hypotheses with the cases of Somaliland and Western Sahara shows that the unique case of support for South Sudan statehood was due to its long and bitter history of conflict, to compatible norms and internationalized ethnic politics—particularly with the U.S., as well as the diminished status of Sudan in the eyes of the international community, especially with regard to human rights violations in Darfur and the security and stability interests triggered by September 11, 2001. The remaining two hypotheses—agreed framework and commitment of the local population, along with economic benefits—appear not to be unique to the case of

South Sudan since the agreed framework was present for both South Sudan and Western Sahara and commitment of the local population was present in all three cases. The second factor (economic benefits) is particularly relevant to Western Sahara, since the U.S. and France have an interest in Morocco's resources and hence are less interested in Saharawi's independence.

1. Introduction

——◦◦——

THE BIRTH OF ANY state in the world is influenced by other nation-states that have both political and economic power. Political power distinguishes the regional from the great powers since the latter determines international influence in secessions and recognition of states. Although secession is not a new phenomenon in international and comparative politics, the end of the Cold War has made it a critical area of research with the dissolution of the USSR and of Yugoslavia. This is not to dispute the fact that secession is as old as history and began in 933 BCE when the tribes of northern Israel seceded from the 'larger Davidian Kingdom' soon after King Solomon died (Siroky, 2009: 2). This theological anecdote serves as the etymology of secession.

While some secession took place in Europe around the 1900s and again during the 1990s, other cases took place in Asia between the 1970s and 1990s and also in Africa in the 1990s. Experiencing the increasing number of secessionist movements in the post-Cold War period, the great powers (U.S., UK, France, Russia and China) reacted in contradictory ways, by supporting and recognizing some cases of secession while neglecting others. Why is this so? Why, for example, did the great powers support the secessions of Timor-Leste and of Eritrea, but not of South Ossetia, Abkhazia or Chechnya? Why did the great powers strongly support the secession of South Sudan but not the cases of Somaliland or Western Sahara? What is so particular about South Sudan that the whole world, led by the enduring great powers, supported its secession and massively recognized it as a sovereign independent state, while its sisters such as Somaliland and Western Sahara, which had sought independence earlier, did not get support?

Is this more to do with the great powers' national interests? Or is it about the perceived stability that the seceding region would bring to the international community? This raises an important theoretical and empirical concern in investigating the great powers' support to secessions and recognition of statehoods and this dissertation seeks to contribute to this debate.

1.1 Structure of the Book

This study relied on elite interviews conducted during short field visits and on secondary sources. It combines process tracing and the comparative method in order to determine how the South Sudan case became so different from the cases of Somaliland and Western Sahara. Because the comparative method shows the existence of causal mechanisms, but not why and how causation occurs, process tracing within case comparisons validates causal chains, causal processes and contextual evidence and is suitable for this research.

I refer in this study to the great powers' support1 for secession and recognition, as influenced by the U.S. and Western European countries. I shall argue that the domestic and international environment of the seceding region determines the level of support from the great powers. The argument of this book is outlined as follows: Section One introduces the research question and methodology, while Section Two discusses the concept of secession, the norms of sovereignty and the realist theory. Section Three accounts for the selection of cases and sets out arguments for why the South Sudan secession was strongly supported. I shall examine competing arguments concerning domestic and international factors to account for the support to South Sudan's secession. In doing so, I shall test hypotheses such as: the history of conflict; the existence of agreed framework and the commitment of the

---

1   Support for secession refers to pre-secession and secession assistance and recognition rendered by great powers.

local population; the existence of compatible norms and internationalized ethnic politics; the status of the mother state in the eyes of the international community; the economic benefits, and the security and stability interest. I shall then situate these hypotheses within a baseline comparison with Somaliland and Western Sahara in order to determine which amongst these six hypotheses if any is (are) unique and stands to explain the great powers' support for South Sudan's secession. Section Four discusses and presents the valid hypotheses according to the empirical literature and elite interviews and Section Five concludes with a summary of my arguments and a direction for further research.

2. The Concept of Seccession

⸺◦⸺

MANY POLITICAL SCIENTISTS and legal scholars have defined and explained secession at length. There have been scholarly spats about which definition should be adopted and which should not. James Crawford defines it as "… the creation of a state by the use or threat of force without the consent of the former sovereignty" (Crawford, 2006: 375). Julie Dahlitz defines it as follows: "The issue of secession arises whenever a significant proportion of the population of a given territory, being part of a state, expresses the wish by word or by deed to become a sovereign state in itself or to join and become part of another sovereign state" (Dahlitz, 2003: 6).

However, the definition of Aleksander Pavkovic and Peter Radan is relevant to the broader debate of this book. They define secession as "a process of withdrawal of a territory and its population from an existing state and the creation of a new state on that territory" (Pavkovic and Radan, 2007: 4). They further note that secession is complete when it leads to recognition of independence. However, when secession does not lead to statehood then it becomes only attempted secession. Although the argument of Pavkovic and Radan is robust, it concentrates on the substance and not on the pro-cedure of secession. Achieving secession is an important goal, but how it is achieved is even more important. In setting out the procedure of secession, Woodrow Wilson, in his seminal fourteen points speech dubbed the "principle(s) of national self-determination", contends that the procedure of secession must be:

Based upon a strict observance of the principle that in determining all such questions of sovereignty, the interests of the populations concerned must have equal weight with the equitable claims of the government whose title is to be determined (Woodrow, 1918: 680-681).

Wilson argued for the principle of self-determination to be "people-driven" and the 1919 Paris Peace Accord defined 'people' as the "ethnic groups that had become nationally mobilized, and numerous states that were carved out of the ruins of the Russian, German, Austro-Hungarian, and Ottoman empires along broadly ethnic lines" (Moore, 2003: 3). These divisions led to the polarization of ethnic groups into many small sub-ethnic societies and later ended by encouraging various regions to pursue secession.

As a result, the increase in demand resulted into the enshrining of principles in the states' constitutions. For example, the principle of national self-determination was recognized in the Soviet constitution in the 1920s and consequently recognized as an international law in the 1960s. Although the right of self-determination became a crucial factor in the procedure of secession, not all secessionists followed internationally agreed procedures, and many ended up by making unilateral declarations of independence. However, groups that seek special status, increased autonomy and additional civil rights short of formal government separation are not secessionists, even if their message is nationalist (Bridget, 2006: 54). Equally, groups that seek to overthrow a regime, carry out revolutions or need to join other states are not secessionists but state reformers.

After having seceded, a group or region may need recognition in order to engage with the international system. How can sovereignty be conferred on a region that has seceded?

2.1 Norms of Sovereignty

Andreas Osiander and Stephen Krasner are the two widely
known scholars who have worked on the conceptualization of
sovereignty. Although the two are seen as sceptical with regard
to the concept, they nonetheless provide an insight into the
practice. Krasner outlines four understandings of sovereignty:

*International legal sovereignty, referring to the practice as-
sociated with mutual recognition, Westphalia sovereignty,
referring to the political organization based on the exclusion of external actors, Domestic sovereignty, referring to
the formal organization of political authority and interde-
pendence sovereignty, referring to the ability of public authorities to control border movements (Krasner, 1999: 4).*

All these definitions give a nuanced understanding of the ap-
plicability of sovereignty. However, since this essay is focusing

on support for secession, then international legal sovereignty becomes more important for explaining why some states are recognized while others are not.

Krasner argues that the basic guidelines for recognition have not been applied equally to all states and governments. Instead, Krasner contends that mutual recognition has been anchored in interests of the great powers and institutions. He acknowledges that governments and regions that should have been recognized have not been and that international institutions such as the World Trade Organization have instead given status to entities such as Hong Kong, even though they do not possess the legal status of a sovereign state (Krasner, 1999:16). Furthermore, during the opening ceremonies of the 2012 Olympic Games in London, the Olympic committee recognized secessionist movements such as Palestine and Taiwan as entities although these are not legally recognized sovereign states. This makes scholars question if sovereignty could be granted to self-claimed autonomous entities and

Andreas Siander argues "it was not realized, far from being traditional, this ideology had its roots only in the transient nineteenth-century heyday of state autonomy" (Siander, 2001: 282). Whether or not this would provide an explanation for the recognition of South Sudan in terms of the shared sovereignty with Sudan stipulated by the 2005 Comprehensive Peace Agreement (CPA), the extension of diplomatic recognition has not been legally premised, but politically motivated. This makes Krasner view "sovereignty as hypocrisy and in practice affords few of the protections that it promotes in principle" (Krasner, 1999: 7).

But why is recognition important? Krasner further notes that recognition can pave the way for membership of international organizations, some of which provide financial aid, as well as facilitate the conclusion of treaties and increase domestic political support (Krasner, 1999: 223). The appeal of becoming a fully-fledged member of the United Nations can lead to economic and security benefits for a state (ibid: 18).

But what is important to keep in mind is the inconsistent application of international legal sovereignty. For example, a state that may meet international legal requirements, such as Somaliland, was not recognized; however, Eritrea was recognized by the international community but did not meet basic governance criteria. Krasner then views international legal sovereignty as having "clear logics of appropriateness, but these logics are sometimes inconsistent with logic of consequences. Given the absence of authoritative institutions and power asymmetries, rulers can follow logic of consequences and reject logic of appropriateness. So, principles have been enduring but violated" (Krasner, 1999: 40).

From such an analysis, it appears that sovereignty does not follow clearly laid down norms. So why did the great powers confer sovereignty on South Sudan?

2.2 Realist Theory

Hans J. Morgenthau, recognized as the father of international relations coined the realist theory. Known as political realism, the realist theory's central argument is that states' interaction in the international system is based on national interest and security rather than ideals. The main signpost that helps political realism to find its way through the landscape of international politics is the concept of interest defined in terms of power (Morgenthau, 2006: 5). This theory helps to explain why some secessions like the case of South Sudan, were strongly supported while others such as those of Western Sahara and Somaliland were not. States will engage the international system in a zero-sum game to maximize their own power and prevent international anarchy. In maximizing their power and interests, the weakest states will "have a say" while the strongest states will "have their way". This means that the great powers will use their economic and political might to rally support for an ally's secession and the conferring of recognition and withhold those of a non-ally, no matter how genuine the case.

Although the great powers' support for secession may be determined by their own national interest, they will also observe certain prerequisites that a seceding region should fulfil in order for it to be supported and recognized as a state. The Montevideo Convention on the Rights and Duties of States of 1933 states as conditions that a region must have:[2]

- A permanent population;
- A defined territory;
- Government;
- And capacity to enter into relations with the other states.

What is interesting is that, even though the Montevideo Convention stipulates such clear prerequisites, not all seceding regions that fulfil these conditions come to be recognized. For

2   See: http://www.jus.uio.no/english/services/library/treaties/01/1-02/rights-duties-states.xml

example, South Sudan and Somaliland both met these conditions, but Somaliland was not recognized. Western Sahara is
close to meeting them but failed to be recognized. This shows
that the national interests of great powers are more important
than mere fulfilment by a region or people of the Montevideo
Convention. So, various strategies of the great powers will determine the viability of new states in the international community.

To be sure, many domestic movements believe that they
can operate as sovereign states, but "without any formal recognition even the most internally organized seceded region
cannot be considered as a sovereign state" (Strang, 1990:
149). Thus, a unilateral declaration of independence has
no value in the international community if it fails to attract
support from other states. It is important to argue that all
foreign recognition or support for secession does not carry
equal weight politically. An act of recognition conferred by a
major power has a greater impact on the process of secession
than recognition granted by a weaker state (Paquin, 2004: 2).

Support for secession from a number of great powers is just as important as from one or two power states. Combined power in the international system rings out when world superpowers, under the stewardship of the U.S., extends recognition to a new state.

Although the motives of great powers to support secessions and for recognition have always remained their own with much resting on the domestic and international environment of a seceding region. I now turn to case studies and to the testing of competing arguments (hypotheses).

3. Case Studies and Competing Arguments

—◦◦—

3.1 Selection of Cases

I SELECTED SOMALILAND and Western Sahara as my baseline comparisons with South Sudan. Somaliland and Western Sahara are struggling African regions that share a similar history with South Sudan. For example, the history of conflict with their home governments is a common historical denominator for all three cases. Moreover, the history of colonialism clusters them together. Although South Sudan was colonized as part of Greater Sudan by Britain, Somaliland by Britain and Western Sahara by Spain, these three cases share a history of conquest and colonial legacies. In terms of difference, South Sudan is predominantly a Christian and animist region, while Somaliland and Western Sahara are predominantly Islamic regions. By using these cases, it will be important to determine why the South Sudan case is unique and what interests benefited the great powers, isolating it from these two other African cases.

3.1.1 South Sudan

South Sudan, officially known as the Republic of South Sudan, is a land-locked country in East and Central Africa. It is bordered to the east by Ethiopia, to the north by Sudan, to the west by the Central Africa Republic, to the southwest by Democratic Republic of Congo, to the south by Uganda, and to the southeast by Kenya.

It gained independence from the Republic of the Sudan in 2011, making it the most recent sovereign state or country with widespread recognition. Its capital and largest city is Juba.

It includes the vast swamp region of the Sudd formed by the White Nile and known locally as the Bahr el Jebel meaning "Mountain River". Sudan was occupied by Egypt under the Muhammed Ali dynasty and was governed as an Anglo-Egyptian condominium until Sudanese independence in January 1956. Following the First Sudanese civil war, the Southern Sudan Autonomous Region was formed in 1972 and lasted until 1983.

A second civil war championed by the SPLM/A broke out and ended in 2005 with the Comprehensive Peace Agreement (CPA). Later that year, southern autonomy was restored when an autonomous Government of Southern Sudan (GoSS) was formed. South Sudan became an independent state on 9 July 2011, following 98.83% support for independence in an internationally supervised referendum (Chol, 2012). It has suffered ethnic violence, endured a civil war characterized by widespread human rights abuses, including various ethnic massacres and killing of human rights activists by all sides from 2013 until September 2018. When South Sudan rivals Salva Kiir Mayardit and Riek Machar Teny struck a unity deal they formed a coalition government, paving the way for refugees to return home.

South Sudan has a population of 12 million, mostly of the Nilotic peoples, and it is demographically among the youngest nations in the world, with roughly half under 18 years old (UNDP, 2013). The majority of inhabitants adhere to Christianity or various Indigenous faiths.

The country is a 193rd member of United Nations (UN), the 54th member the African Union (AU), the sixth member of East African Community (EAC), and the eighth member of Intergovernmental Authority on Development (IGAD) and is a party to the Geneva Conventions. As of 2019, South Sudan ranks the third lowest in the latest UN World Happiness Report, the second lowest on the Global Peace Index, the last in Transparency International Corruption Index for 2020 and has the third-highest score on the American Funds for Peace's Fragile States.

3.1.2 Somaliland

Somaliland is officially the Republic of Somaliland. It is a self-declared State in the Horn of Africa, internationally considered to be part of Federal Republic of Somalia. The government of Somaliland regards itself as the successor state to British Somaliland, which, as the briefly independent State of Somaliland united in 1960 with the Trust Territory of Somaliland (the former Italian Somaliland) to form the Somali Republic.

Somaliland lies in the Horn of Africa, on the southern coast of the Gulf of Aden. It is bordered by Djibouti to the northwest, Ethiopia to the south and west, and Somalia to the east. Its claimed territory has an area of 176,120 square kilometers (68,000 sq. m), with approximately 3.5 million residents in 2014 (Mahamood, 2019). The capital and largest city is Hargeisa.

In 1988, the Siad Barre government began a crackdown

against the Hargeisa-based Somali National Movement (SNM) and other militant groups, which were among the events that led to the Somali Civil War. The conflict left the country's economic and military infrastructure severely damaged. Following the collapse of Barre's government in early 1991, local authorities, led by the SNM, unilaterally declared independence from Somalia on 18 May of the same year and reinstated the borders of the former short-lived independent State of Somaliland.

Since 1991, the territory has been governed by democratically elected governments that seek international recognition of its secession as the Government of the Republic of Somaliland. The central government maintains foreign relations of Somaliland with some foreign governments, who have sent delegations to Hargeisa. Ethiopia also maintains a trade office in the region. However, Somaliland's self-proclaimed independence has not been officially recognized by any country or international organization. It is a member of the Unrepresented

Nations and Peoples Organization (UNPO), an advocacy group whose members consist of indigenous peoples, minorities and unrecognized or occupied territories.

3.1.3 Western Sahara

Western Sahara is a disputed territory on the northwest coast and in the Maghreb region of North and West Africa About 20% of the territory is controlled by the self-proclaimed Sahrawi Arab Democratic Republic, while the remaining 80% of the territory is occupied and administered by neighboring Morocco (Sarama, 2020). Its surface area amounts to 266,000 square kilometers (103,000 sq m) (ibid). It is one of the most sparsely populated territories in the world, mainly consisting of desert flatlands. The population is estimated at just over 500,000, of which nearly 40% live in Laayoune, the largest city in Western Sahara (Anderson, 2020).

Occupied by Spain until 1975, Western Sahara has been on the United Nations list of non-self-governing territories since 1963 after a Moroccan demand. It is the most populous territory on that list, and by far the largest in area. In 1965, the United Nations General Assembly adopted its first resolution on Western Sahara, asking Spain to decolonize the territory. One year later, a new resolution was passed by the General Assembly requesting that a referendum be held by Spain on self-determination. In 1975, Spain relinquished the administrative control of the territory to a joint administration by Morocco (which had formally claimed the territory since 1957) and Mauritania.

A war erupted between those countries and a Sahrawi nationalist movement, the Polisario Front, which proclaimed the Sahrawi Arab Democratic Republic (SADR) with a government in exile in Tindouf, Algeria. Mauritania withdrew its claims in 1979, and Morocco eventually secured de facto control of most of the territory, including all the major cities and natural resources. The United Nations considers the Polisario Front to be the legitimate representative of the

Sahrawi people, and maintains that the Sahrawis have a right to self-determination.

Since a United Nations-sponsored ceasefire agreement in 1991, two-thirds of the territory (including most of the Atlantic coastline—the only part of the coast outside the Moroccan Western Sahara Wall is the extreme south, including the Ras Nouadhibou Peninsula) has been administered by the Moroccan government, with tacit support from France and the U.S., and the remainder by the SADR, backed by Algeria. Internationally, countries such as Russia have taken an ambiguous and neutral position on each side's claims and have pressed both parties to agree on a peaceful resolution. Both Morocco and Polisario have sought to boost their claims by accumulating formal recognition, especially from African, Asian and Latin American states in the developing world. The Polisario Front has won formal recognition for SADR from 46 states and was extended membership in the African Union (Muhammad, 2019). Morocco has won support for its position from several African governments and from most of the Muslim world and Arab League. In both instances, recognitions have, over the past two decades, been extended and withdrawn back and forth, depending on the development of relations with Morocco.

Until 2017, no other member state of the United Nations had ever officially recognized Moroccan sovereignty over parts of Western Sahara but a number of countries have expressed their support for a future recognition of the Moroccan annexation of the territory as an autonomous part of the kingdom. In 2020, the U.S. recognized Moroccan sovereignty over Western Sahara in exchange for Moroccan normalization of relations with Israel.

In 1984, the African Union's predecessor, the Organization of African Unity, recognized the Sahrawi Arab Democratic Republic as one of its full members, with the same status as Morocco, and Morocco protested by suspending its membership to the OAU. Morocco was readmitted into the

African Union on 30 January 2017 by ensuring that the conflicting claims between Morocco and the SADR would be solved peacefully and stopping the extension of its exclusive military control by building additional walls. Until their conflict is resolved, the African Union has not issued any formal statement about the border separating the sovereign territories of Morocco and the SADR in Western Sahara. Instead, the African Union participates with the United Nations mission, in order to maintain a ceasefire and reach a peace agreement between its two members. The African Union provides peacekeeping contingent to the UN mission, which is deployed to control a buffer zone near the de facto border of walls, built by Morocco within Western Sahara.

3.2 Competing Arguments of Successful and Failed Secessions

3.2.1 Domestic Factors

History of Conflict

The history of conflict in Sudan is viewed through the lenses of identity and marginalization. Francis Deng provides a comprehensive background of ethnic identity. He views identity as social dimension and argues that it is a *"set of persons marked by a label and distinguished by implicit or explicit rules and characteristics such as beliefs, desires, moral commitments, race, gender, ethnicity, religion, language, and culture"* (Deng, 1995:1). He contends that ethnic identities were strong in Sudan with Arabs regarding themselves as a superior race while regarding black Africans as less worthy (ibid: 3). This tendency led to a slave trade during the periods of Turco-Egyptian rule (1821-1884), Mahidiya rule (1885-1899), and the Anglo-Egyptian rule (1899-1956). The people involved of course could have been Europeans, Turks, Egyptians, Arabs or any other light-skinned race which took part in the raiding expeditions for slaves that afflicted the area from the earliest recorded times (Deng, 2009: 29). The British Imperialist rulers abolished the slave trade in 1834.

Furthermore, the imposition of Arab and Islamic culture explains another strand of conflict of identity as Christian Knox argues: "In particular, it was the imposition of Arab, Islamic identity by the government in Khartoum that caused decades of alienation among many Sudanese living in the South who primarily thought of themselves as African and either Christians or belonging to traditional African religions" (Knox, 2012: 16). As a result, Southern Sudan was isolated and cut off from Sudan in terms of development. Douglas Johnson argues that the southern region was a closed off part of Sudan (Johnson, 2012: 1). The area, according to him, was like a 'tribal zoo' (ibid: 1). Johnson further notes that the introduction of Native Administration by

Anglo-Egyptians made Southern Sudan a backward region. This new system of Native Administration in the South was further reinforced by the Closed Districts Ordinance, first introduced in 1922, which prevented Southerners from accessing development opportunities (Johnson, 2012: 1). However, in reaction to such policies, the South Sudanese waged two civil wars against the oppressive northern regime. In 1955, the first "Anyanya One" war, fought by Southern Sudanese rebels against the Khartoum government, was an expression of rebellion against exclusion, neglect, persecution and the trading of Southerners as slaves. This traditional war halted with the signing of the 1972 Addis Ababa peace Agreement, which promised a right of self-determination to the Southern Sudanese. Lacking international backing, the Addis Ababa Agreement was abrogated ten years later by President Jaafar Nimeiry, asserting that it respected neither the Koran nor the Bible (Alier 2003: 102). This action led to a second war in 1983, which "claimed an estimated two million lives, injured millions, displaced four million people, created immeasurable vulnerabilities and plunged the region into further degradation" (Lokosang, 2010: 18).

It is against such a historical account of conflict that some of the great powers and influential actors such as the U.S., UK and Norway, became known as the "Troika", as well as friends of the Sudanese peace process amongst other partners, began the search for peace in Sudan. The result of their efforts was the Comprehensive Peace Agreement (CPA), signed in 2005, which recognized the right of self-determination, and paved the way for the secession of South Sudan.

In contrast, Somaliland's history of conflict is not as severe as that of South Sudan. Somali conflicts were viewed not through ethnic identity or marginalization lenses but as clan disputes. The history goes back to the union of British Somaliland with Italian Somalia to form the Republic of Somalia in 1960. Of course, the 1969 coup, staged by Major General Mohammed Siad Barre, posed a great influence in

Somali politics. However, by the 1990s the moral authority of Barre's Daarooq clan government had collapsed, leading to the Somali civil war (Roble, 2007: 12). This war, carried out by militia groups of the Isaaq clan and, led by the Somali National Movement (SNM) based in Hargeisa, caused an estimated 10,000 deaths (ibid: 12). Several months later, the SNM declared the independence of the northern Somaliland territory. The commonly argued reason for the commencement of civil war and unilateral declaration of independence (UDI) by the northern Somalilanders has been the assertion of the Somali state's collapse driven by economic crisis. The Isaaq clan elites wanted to control the new economy in this independent state and to directly benefit from its commerce.

However, because of the common language, culture and religion shared by the people of Somaliland and Somalia, and with no ethnic discrimination and major atrocities committed between the two regions, the great powers viewed it as unnecessary to recognize Somaliland as a sovereign state and instead regarded this as the African Union's affair.

Western Sahara's history of conflict is also not as protracted as that of South Sudan. Although it had the 1975-1991 war with Morocco that led to the death of 14,000 to 21,000 people from both sides, the destruction of war is not as severe as the Sudanese civil wars. Moreover, Western Sahara shared Arab ethnicity with those of Morocco. Having been a Spanish colony from 1884 to 1975, Western Sahara was to be granted independence in 1975, but Morocco and Mauritania approached the International Court of Justice and interpreted its ruling as supporting their historical claims to the territory (Jensen, 2012: 2). However, Mauritania relinquished its claims on Western Sahara and Morocco took control. Angered by this move, the Polisario Front unilaterally declared Western Sahara an independent state and to be known as the Saharawi Arab Democratic Republic. The Polisario Front later agreed to pursue peaceful negotiations, which have reached a cul-de-sac on the issue of a referendum. Thus, the history of conflict was rooted in power struggles and not based on ethnicity. Therefore, on the basis of its single ethnicity and culture, the great powers have viewed the issue of Saharawi's independence as less grievous and urgent than that of South Sudan. I now turn to examining agreed framework and commitment of local population.

Agreed Framework and Commitment of Local Population

Support for South Sudanese secession can be explained from the perspective of the framework of the Comprehensive Peace Agreement (CPA), which stipulated the right of self-determination of the people of South Sudan and thus their right to either confirm unity or opt for secession. The Machakos Protocol, Article 1.3, states that "the people of South Sudan have the right to self-determination, inter alia, through a referendum to determine their future status" (Dau, 2011: 48). Most of the great powers influenced the implementation of CPA. The "Troika" put pressure on Sudanese government and rallied support from their allies for the timely holding of the referendum vote and further recognition of the independence of South Sudan. Of course, the high level of international participation in the crafting of the CPA, which led to secession, meant that the global community was willing to recognize the new nation as soon as it declared independence (Knox, 2012: 47).

In contrast, Somaliland's secession did not follow any agreed framework, such as the right of self-determination for the declaration of independence in 1991. Although the 2001 constitutional referendum is referenced by Somaliland scholars as having been successful and an indication in favour of recognition, this was a constitutional dispensation that carried no weight of statehood. Conversely, the 1991 declaration of independence can be viewed as a confirmation of the June 1960 independence of Somaliland from Britain, which originally separated Somaliland from Somalia. However, a voluntary "Act of Union" between the two countries seems to carry legal weight and negates the 1991 withdrawal and declaration of Somaliland statehood. Moreover, the 1991 UDI appeared impromptu and lacked a consensus among all clans. There exists a wide claim that independence was an interest of the Isaaq clan. However, Ali Ismael argues that, although the Isaaq clan comprises sub-clans such as the Garhajis, Habar Awal and Habar Jelo, the Garhajis, the largest and most powerful sub-clan, was against secession (Ismael, 2002: 2).

On the other hand, the Western Sahara case challenges the agreed-framework argument. Although Western Sahara's secession was detailed in the United Nations Organization of African Unity framework, which later became the UN Settlement Plan, allowing Saharawi's to exercise their right of self-determination through a referendum. The question of who was eligible to vote caused a stalemate and as a result, the Moroccan government disputed the referendum. However, the great powers showed no interest in putting pressure on both parties, showing that the agreed-framework argument is a necessary, but not sufficient, prerequisite for support for secession.

Whereas agreed framework can be a step forward, advocacy for independence becomes more important. In the case of South Sudan's secession, the commitment of the local population also played a critical role. Seven months before the referendum, campaigns for independence were spread across South Sudan. Dr. Cirino Hiteng termed the role played by youth in educating and campaigning for secession as a 'unique sense of nationalism' (Hiteng, 2012). Moreover, Hon. Michael Makuei contended that the South Sudanese, at civil society and government levels, had chosen independence even before the poll (Makuei, 2012). While the campaigns were reported as 'all citizens for secession', the local and international media picked this up as the sole choice of the people of South Sudan. This challenges Ivor Jennings' assertion that "people cannot decide unless someone decides who the people are" (Jennings, 1956: 5).

Certainly, the organization of such nationwide demonstrations was perhaps motivated by the unity of all 63 sub-ethnic groups and their political elites. One of the possible avenues for such unity was perhaps the 'All Southern Sudanese Political Parties Conference' held in October 2010, which later agreed a message of unity of 23 political parties for the secession of South Sudan (LoWilla, 2012). As argued by Dankwart Rustow, national unity implies nothing mysterious about daily pledges of allegiance, about personal identity in the psychoanalyst's sense, or about a grand political purpose pursued by the citizenry as a whole (Rustow, 1970: 350). As the referendum drew nearer, many opinion polls revealed the massive support for independence. The Agency for Independent Media (AIM) released its opinion polls on 16 September 2010 in Juba showing 96% of South Sudanese as supporting independence[3]. Convinced by opinion polls, the

3   Conducted by AIM : http://www.sudanradio.org/opin-ion-poll-suggests-96-percent-vote-secession-says

U.S. Deputy Chief of Mission in Juba acknowledged "our support to South Sudan's secession was motivated by the overwhelming decision of the people of South Sudan several months before referendum polls day" (Datta, 2012: 23).

In the case of Somaliland, there was a local population commitment to independence though not through domestic street demonstrations as in the case of South Sudan, but through diaspora community campaigns. Domestic participation was affected by disunity amongst the clans, sub-clans and political elites, as argued earlier. This problem emanated from a lack of a strong political centre that could bring all the clans together. The advantage that Southern Sudan had over Somaliland was an interim semi-autonomous government that embraced all ethnic groups under 10 decentralized state governments.

Western Sahara also had a local population commitment for independence yet still failed to attract the great powers' support. For example, several protests and campaigns carried out by Saharawi did not influence the U.S. and its Western allies to support independence. One of the memorable demonstrations was the Gdeim Lzik protest of November 2009, which mobilized over 500 Saharawi demanding independence, but which later ended with hundreds of deaths and hundreds arrested by the Moroccan authorities (Bahaijoub, 2010: 269). This therefore negates the argument of local population commitment, showing this as a necessary, but not a sufficient, prerequisite of support from the great powers to secessions. I now turn to an examination of international factors.

3.2.2 International Factors

Compatible Norms and Internationalized Ethnic Politics
Moral and cultural sociologists argue that shared values and ethnic relations cement ties and cooperation. The case of South Sudan's successful secession can be attributed to a sharing of values such as religious beliefs and linguistic association with

Western countries. It is plausible to argue that the majority of the Western powers, under leadership of the U.S., are predominately Christian states. South Sudan, which is mainly a Christian region, marshalled support for its independence on these grounds. The bedrock of such support was seen through the activism of Western churches. For example, both U.S. evangelical churches and Christian solidarity advocated the ending of slavery and of the plight of the Southern Sudanese through peace in Sudan (Madut, 2012). The influence of the traditional evangelical community was so immense in U.S. politics that when Bush was elected in 2004, 78% of his votes came from evangelicals (Halton, 2007: 4). Hence the evangelical movements and other Christian activists, maintaining the same political influence, convinced the U.S. government to intercede on behalf of South Sudan. Allen Hertzke, in his Annual Paul Henry's Lecture, argued:

Due to the activists' pressured on the U.S. government; the Sudan peace accord was made lawful by enactment of the Sudan Peace Act 2002, which plucked the tragedy of Sudan from the backwaters of international concern. Long before the current crisis in Darfur, and long before September 11th 2001, highlighted the threat of militant Islamic ideology, Christian solidarity activists and their Jewish allies sounded the alarm about the genocidal aims of Khartoum's self-described Jihad against its African population - a population made up of tribal religionists, Christians and non-militant Muslims. (Hertzke, 2004: 3).

Although religion may appear to be an important social tie, the adoption of linguistic enclaves, such as English as an official language of South Sudan, increased the motivation for supporting its secession. However, Somaliland also adopted English as its official language yet failed to gain recognition. The migration patterns of the South Sudanese could have perhaps strengthened support for South Sudan's secession. Many South Sudanese sought asylum in the U.S. and the resettlement of 3500 South Sudanese 'lost boys' and lost girls' during the civil war deepened the affinity between the two nations, despite distance (Avlon, 2011: 1). The 'lost boys and girls' increased Western countries' understanding of the conflicts and civil wars in Sudan.

Apart from these social ties, ethnic politics has increasingly been regarded as a central element in support for secession from third party states. Saideman (1997: 724) argues, for instance, that states support the side in an ethnic conflict that includes the leaders' constituents. He further asserts that "ethnic politics serves as a critical dynamic compelling some politicians to support secession elsewhere while constraining others" (Saideman, 1997: 725-726). In the U.S., for example, the tri-partisan coalition of the Black Caucus, the Sudan Caucus and the Jewish Zionist movements was seen as having championed the cause of supporting South Sudanese black

Africans' freedom. Crucially viewed as the peak of American support of South Sudanese, numerous congressmen such as Frank Wolf, Michael Capuano and the late Donald Payne advocated for South Sudan's independence. In 1989, Rep. Wolf travelled into the war-ravaged terrain of Southern Sudan to become the first U.S. representative to meet with the head of the Southern Sudanese rebels, the late John Garang (Hamilton, 2011: 1). Payne, a black congressman, followed a few years later, and on his return to Washington pushed for the U.S. House of Representatives to pass a resolution endorsing the right of the Southern Sudanese to exercise self-determination (ibid: 1). Although these three played leading roles, there were others who also supported the South Sudanese underground. "Behind all this was [and] still is, a small group of people who have been working behind the scenes for almost 20 years to make this independence a success", a senior member of the U.S. government remarked during the proclamation of South Sudan's independence (Hamilton, 2011: 1).

In contrast Somaliland is predominately Muslim. It is arguable that the great powers, which are in their majority Christian states, could not support Somaliland's secession, because religious groups such as the traditional evangelical movements and Christian solidarity activists in the U.S. would mostly be motivated to champion the Christians' cause. This also applies in the case of Western Sahara, which is preponderantly an Islamic region. Although both Somaliland and Western Sahara had large diaspora communities, they did not have dedicated congressmen like Wolf, Capuano and Payne who could champion their cause. I now turn to examining the status of the mother state.

Status of Mother State in the Eyes of the International Community
The case of South Sudan's successful secession is due to the status of Sudan in the eyes of peaceful States. Sudan has a tainted image in the eyes of Western powers. For instance, the wide-scale abuse of human rights and poor governance

had continued unabated. The Darfur crisis only served to further delegitimize the Al-Bashir government in the eyes of the international community and crucially the Southern Sudanese (Knox, 2012: 35). Because of the Darfur crisis, the International Criminal Court (ICC) indicted and issued arrest warrants for President Al-Bashir and some senior members of his government on charges of war crimes, crimes against humanity and genocide. This not only showcased Khartoum as an irresponsible government, but also compelled the West to impose sanctions and isolated Sudan from international engagement. With the Darfur crisis and other abuses of human rights, pressure mounted on the West to stand with South Sudan. Thus, most Western advocates could feel the intensity of Sudanese government actions. Richard Cockett argues that "the Sudanese government virtually broke off any reasonable cooperation with the West over the South, Darfur or anywhere else. Instead, it cultivated a sense of betrayal and suspicion" (Cockett, 2010: 242). The international community realized that Al-Bashir could not necessary be trusted and the perception of ethnic persecution probably tipped sympathies toward the Southern rebels (Knox, 2012: 43).

In contrast to Western Sahara, Morocco was found to be a friendly state in the eyes of the international community. The appearance of Morocco as a moderate Islamic kingdom that embraced democracy, respect for human rights and with a new constitution that made it a constitutional monarchy, made the great powers shun the Polisario Front's demand for secession. In any case, the great powers considered that Western Sahara would be an unviable state, given the action of Unilateral Declaration of Independence (UDI) in 1976 by a less than organized Polisario leadership. The eligibility to vote in the Western Saharan referendum is a strategic stalemate of the great powers, which foresaw chaos in a state with a population of 500,000 and with three-quarters of these numbers still refugees in Algeria (Jensen, 2012: 52). Such delaying tactics show how much more important Morocco's role is in the

Arab Maghreb Union than that of Western Sahara. The great powers preferred Western Sahara to become an autonomous state in Morocco, but not a sovereign state (Bahaijoub, 2010: 285).

In the case of Somaliland, the great powers were only able to maintain the status quo. Both self-declared Somaliland and Somalia are viewed as unviable states, according to the great powers' assessment. Although numerous scholars have praised Somaliland as a democratic, inclusive and functioning state, issues of human rights have continued to raise doubts about its recognition. A good example is the arrest and jailing of the Qaran leadership, the deportation of Mr. Jaam'a M. Qaalib, a leading unionist, from his own home region and the rape of the young Daarood girl, Zamzam Du'aale (Roble, 2007: 10). Although Somaliland can be taken as a more functioning state than the failed Somalia, it will continue to be assessed for the positive role it can play in the international community given the unlawful UDI. Therefore, recognition of Somaliland's independence has been referred to African Union's recognition, which is unlikely to be granted. The AU's lack of commitment to recognizing Somaliland's independence is based on the assumption that there will be chaos if colonial boundaries are not observed in post-independence Africa (Mail and Guardian online, 2006: 1). However, this was not a condition for Eritrea or South Sudan. I now turn to an examination of economic benefits.

Economic Benefits

Resource wealth has been debated by both comparative politics and international relations scholars as a motivation for support for secessions and recognition. Scholars such as David Gibbs for example have argued that American private interest influences U.S. foreign policy. He asserts "politicians and businesspeople act rationally to further their respective self-interests and such rational behaviour influences the conduct of U.S. foreign policy" (Gibbs, 1991: 33). Using the

'Business Conflict Model', Gibbs assumes that economic groups compete on the basis of their different interests, which they struggle to maximize every day. He justifies the argument of the U.S. resources interest on the basis of the 1960 Congo crisis, pointing out that Washington was divided into two economic interests groups; those that supported the Katanga secession so that they could take over Belgian industrial concessions, and those that had ties with Brussels decided to support a united Congo. Although his analysis may be plausible, it is limited in validity as applied to the Congo case study. However, this does not negate the assumption that each Western power's economic interest could be unique.

The case of South Sudan deserves critical evaluation since the country is rich in oil and other mineral resources. Although South Sudan has a limited number of Western oil companies, it is arguable that its resource abundance perhaps played a critical role in its swift recognition. The first presence of the French based Total Oil Company, which had some concessions in the Upper Nile region, and the former activities of the British White Nile Company may be seen as attesting this claim. The Russia state media have claimed that Americans unwavering support was motivated by oil, though no single American oil company currently operates in Sudan. In an article posted in the Sudan Tribune, entitled "Russia claims U.S. interest in S. Sudan motivated by oil", Toby Collins quoted KZ Russian state media as claiming "U.S. backed up South Sudan secession and offers it military support because it wants the nascent state's oil" (Sudan Tribune, 16/01/2012). However, a number of Eastern companies have already shown interest in the nascent nation rich resources. Toby Collins further exhibits "Western companies' almost absolute control over the oil resources of the country is less plausible as the dominance of the Sudanese and South Sudanese oil sectors by Eastern companies is well documented" (Sudan Tribune, 16/01/2012). This assertion demonstrates that Sudan and South Sudan oil concessions have been largely dominated by China and Malaysia, with a few concessions to Japan, India and Indonesia.

Further contesting the notion that Western support for South Sudan secession was oil motivated, Jok Madut argues that "support to South Sudanese freedom by Western great powers had nothing to do with oil interests; it was basically on humanity, the history and suffering of people of Southern Sudan" (Madut, 2012). Madut's argument can be continued to note that if the Western great powers' support was oil-motivated, they would have sought contracts, in particular for projects such as the recent multi-billion energy project of building a pipeline to transport oil from South Sudan to Kenyan and Djibouti ports for refining, which has been won by Japan. Of equally nuanced importance is a counterfactual understanding that, had support for South Sudan's secession been oil-motivated, then countries like China, Malaysia and India, which won concessions, would have strongly supported it. Given insufficient scholarly support, the case for a causal relationship between support for South Sudan's secession by the Western great powers and oil is feeble. This analysis shows that economic benefits did not play a critical role in support for South Sudan's secession by the Western great powers.

The economic benefits argument is not entirely convincing in regard to Somaliland, as both Hargeisa and Mogadishu lack substantial resources in which the great powers could take an interest. Conversely, in the Western Sahara case, economic benefits can be analysed as what delayed Morocco to conduct referendum for Saharawi's independence. Western great powers such as the U.S. and France are seen as great allies to Morocco because of its endowment in phosphate and agricultural products, amongst other geo-strategic interests. Morocco has a free trade agreement with the U.S. and a unique associate status with the EU, and enjoys a special relationship with Europe through several partnership programs

(BG and SAIS, 2009: 54). This economic relationship makes the West support Morocco, no matter how slow it is in fulfilling the UN settlement plan that stipulates the holding of a referendum for either integration or independence of Western Sahara. Although this UN settlement plan may be seen as backed up by the U.S., this backing may also be seen as strategic balance, so that U.S. interest in Polisario's strongest ally, Algeria, for that country's natural gas, petroleum and petroleum products, cannot be compromised. Algeria is a strong supporter of Western Saharan independence and the richest amongst the Maghreb countries because of its resources, so the U.S. had to maintain a delicate balance on the Western Sahara case. However, U.S. support is tilted towards Morocco, its close Cold-War ally in the region. I now turn to examining the security and stability interests of the great powers.

Security and Stability Interests

Security and stability are important gauges that stipulate

---

4   The Potomac Institute for Policy Studies (BG) and The Conflict Management Program (SAIS)

whether the states support or suppress secessionist movements. The core of this set of influences is the logic of strategy, alliance and enmity (Bridget, 2006: 62). States are thought to use recognition to weaken their adversaries and empower their allies. This stems from the international security environment and the contribution the region seeking sovereignty may be expected to play. The U.S., for example, would want assurance that the secessionist group is able to maintain external and internal stability (Paquin, 2004: 17). If the seceding region has the capability of maintaining internal and external security, then U.S. support is more likely. If it is not the case, U.S. recognition will be denied and the status quo will be maintained (Paquin, 2004: 17). This U.S. security test became stringent with the September 11 2001 terrorist attacks, which prompted the U.S. government to declare "war on terror". Waging war against terrorists led U.S. and Western European governments to promote policies that make it a condition for any emerging state to be a team player for international peace and security. It is perhaps through such security and stability interests that South Sudan's secession attracted overwhelming support from the great powers. Hilde Johnson, in her influential book 'Waging peace in Sudan', argues that the push by 'Troika' for peace in Sudan was strengthened by the September 11 2001 event and President Bush's desire for the U.S. to take a more active part in the peace talks and was clearly leaning towards Southern positions that appeared friendly (Johnson, 2011: 50).

While the George W. Bush administration championed peace in Sudan and right of self-determination to South Sudanese, the Obama administration did more for the conduct of a referendum. The President wrote letters to the nine heads of the strategic African states of Kenya, Uganda, Tanzania, Ethiopia, Egypt, Libya, South Africa, Malawi and Nigeria, pressing diplomatic pressure on Sudan to hold the referendum as stipulated in the CPA. This diplomatic pressure highlights how secession of South Sudan was an American effort.

The U.S. and other Western powers viewed South Sudan as strategic part of East and Central Africa, and as a better option than Khartoum, which had been a sponsor of al-Qaeda and once harboured Osama Bin Laden. Khartoum's human rights abuses included genocide in Darfur and the wars in South Kordofan, Blue Nile and Abyei Area had shaken the Western powers and led them to consider it an unstable state. This confirmed the 1996 United Nations Security Council Resolution 1044, which essentially called Sudan a threat to stability in Africa (Knox, 2012: 39).

As an option for external security and peace, South Sudan was considered by the EU, the U.S., Israel and other states as a potential new corridor for controlling Islamic jihad and terrorist activities in sub-Saharan Africa and the Middle East. Moreover, the U.S. sees South Sudan as an ally that can end Khartoum's policies of supporting the Lord's Resistance Army (LRA) atrocities, a geo-security interest that made Uganda a strong supporter of South Sudan's secession amongst the

Eastern African countries. This U.S. security interest solidified when the key Pentagon officials visited Southern Sudanese Army headquarters in Juba after secession and was further strengthened by the U.S. admission of South Sudan as a friendly buyer of its military weapons (Sudan Tribune, 16/01/2012). Nevertheless, not all U.S allies supported this position. For example, Egypt, a former joint colonial master with Britain in Sudan and ally of the U.S. in North Africa, feared the likely interference of control over the River Nile waters, the source of Egyptian livelihoods, with the independence of South Sudan. Although this state of affairs was worrying for Cairo, they later played an important role in both appeasing the U.S. and South Sudan, while still tilting its support towards Khartoum. Apart from the U.S., the EU has shown specific interest in South Sudan's security. The donation of 12.5 million euros, meant for the security project of Juba's International Airport, attests to this endeavour (Longatti, 2012). This relationship shows how support for South

Sudan's secession was motivated by concerns of security and stability.

In the case of Somaliland, security and stability interests led the great powers not to extend diplomatic recognition. Although the great powers, under U.S. leadership, argued that recognition of Somaliland was an African Union's affair, they were not convinced that stability would prevail in Hargeisa. The AU position has been guided by the 1964 OAU resolution which vowed to prevent change in African colonial borders lest 'opening Pandora's box' that can lead to a domino effect. Interestingly, this was contradicted by the AU's recognition of South Sudan's independence. To be sure, international recognition of Somaliland's independence has been viewed as potentially leading to unilateral declaration of independence of regions such as Awdal, Sool, Sanaag, Cayn and Puntland (Ismael, 2002: 2). However, the entire issue of Somaliland lies within the U.S discretion. The argument of its being AU's affair is a strategy for keeping the issue quiescent. Although there is goodwill from Ethiopia and Britain towards recognizing Somaliland, the U.S. cannot afford to interfere against the Somali government, which is an ally in the U.S. war against Islamic militants in the region, notably the Council of Islamic Courts and the Al-Shabaab terrorist movement (Reynolds, 2008: 2).

The case of Western Sahara seems to resemble the Somaliland situation. The great powers, particularly the EU and the U.S., have special security and stability interests in their relationship with North Africa and the Arab Maghreb Union (AMU), of which Morocco is a key member. Morocco has been firmly allied with the U.S. in its 'war on terror', in military and intelligence matters, and thus a recognized non-NATO ally of the U.S. (Jensen, 2012: 114). This geo-strategic situation of Morocco in the Middle East and the Western Mediterranean has kept the great powers silent in the push for Western Sahara independence. In any case, the instability of Western Sahara brings forth a lot of worries as a special report on Maghreb demonstrates "with substantial land area, a small population and extremely limited resources, the Western Sahara could fall prey to subversion and terrorist groups now operating in the area" (BG and SAIS, 2009: 5). I now turn to discussing and presenting the results of this research.

4. Discussion and Presentation of Results

⸺◦⸺

THIS SECTION DISCUSSES and presents the results of this research into the great powers' support for South Sudan's secession and their low interest in supporting the secession of Somaliland and Western Sahara. After in-depth analysis and testing of hypotheses against the literature and consultation of interviews conducted, some hypotheses regarding support for South Sudan's secession appeared valid while others were not.

4.1 Discussion of the Results

H1: History of Conflict

One valid hypothesis, history of conflict, traces the ethnic discrimination of the South Sudanese as slaves, who were traded by Khartoum's government to Arab and European slave traders. There was also Khartoum government's policy that isolated the southern region from any development, creating what Douglas Johnson called a 'tribal zoo'. The 1972 Addis Ababa Agreement had a clause providing impetus to self-determination. This was later abrogated but remained a precedent for the 2005 peace agreement, which provided self-determination and later led to the referendum. The two wars of 1955-1972 and 1983-2005, costing the lives of more than two million people, and displacing four million, attracted wider sympathy and support for secession. The cases of Somaliland and Western Sahara, although both have a bitter history, could not match the fifty years of classical marginalization and persecution of the South Sudanese, as demonstrated in the literature.

H2: Compatible Norms and Internationalized Ethnic Politics

Another valid hypothesis is that Sudanese conflict has been constantly a war between Muslims in the North and Christians in the South, and a war between black Africans and Arabs as shown in the literature. The North uses Arabic and Sharia law while the South opted for English and secular laws. Since most of the great Western powers are Christian states and embrace secular laws, their churches campaigned for secession. For example, the U.S. evangelical movements and Jewish movements pressured U.S. government to support South Sudanese people in which they shared similar Christian belief systems. Moreover, American legislators, including Black congressman, such as the late Donald Payne, and Sudan Caucus congressmen, such as Frank Wolf and Michael Capuano, influenced the U.S. government to support

South Sudanese secession. Somaliland and Western Sahara are Islamic states/regions, do not have dedicated U.S. black congressmen to push their cases and lack religious ties with Western society.

H3: Status of the Mother State in the Eyes of the International Community

This is a valid hypothesis, as demonstrated by the literature. In the case of South Sudan, the widespread human rights violations committed by the Khartoum regime in Darfur, which have led to accusations of genocide, and the indictment and issuance of an arrest warrant for President Al-Bashir, perhaps made the great powers support South Sudan as an option for greater respect for human rights and freedoms. In the case of Somaliland, the great powers viewed both Mogadishu and Hargeisa as non-viable states since the latter was also involved in human rights violations. The great powers instead supported the Somali government in dealing with the Islamic extremists of Al-Shabaab militants. The case of Western Sahara is the opposite of South Sudan in that, the great powers saw Morocco as a responsible government in the eyes of the international community and hence were not convinced of the need to support Western Sahara.

H4: Security and Stability Interest

This hypothesis is valid, as demonstrated by empirical literature. For the case of South Sudan, the support for secession by the great powers was influenced by the September 11 2001 attack on the U.S., when Khartoum was found to be supporting al-Qaeda terrorist networks and previously had trained and harboured Osama Bin Laden. The great powers then saw South Sudan as an ally in the war against Islamic terrorist groups and the LRA, and thus supporting its secession was strategic. In the case of Somaliland, the great powers could not support secession because they were allied with the Somali government to flush out the elements of Al-Shabaab militias that posed a threat to the Horn of Africa and world at large. The UDI of Somaliland was viewed by the great powers as a precedent for other secessionists within Somalia, should it be supported. In the case of Western Sahara, the great powers had close military and intelligence cooperation with Morocco in the "war on terror" and Western Sahara was viewed as a recruiting base for radical Islamic terrorists and a non-viable state.

H5: Agreed Framework and Commitment of Local Population

This hypothesis is plausible, but not valid, because it does not make South Sudan's secession distinct from those of Somaliland and Western Sahara. Although Somaliland has no legal procedure for its secession, it does have committed citizens, particularly in the diaspora, and this could have led to recognition. Western Sahara has a legal framework: first the award by the International Court of Justice (ICJ) of Polisario territory in 1975 and second the UN Settlement Plan that promised a right of self-determination. However, this still failed to attract support from the great powers, despite Western Sahara's active local population and diaspora groups.

H6: Economic Benefits

This hypothesis is not valid in the case of South Sudan. Empirical evidence shows that the Western great powers have not shown an interest in its oil, particularly not the U.S., which championed independence. Rather, it is China, Japan and Malaysia that have acquired oil contracts even though they did not champion South Sudan's secession. In the case of Somaliland, there are no substantial resources that could have attracted the great powers to Somalia and led to not recognizing Somaliland. However, in the case of Western Sahara there is an obvious motivation of economic benefits since the U.S. and France are linked to Morocco by phosphate and agricultural products thus these would avoid disappointing Morocco. I will now turn to tabulating these analyses using the comparative method.

4.2 Presentation of Results Using Comparative Method

Table 1: Comparison of Three Cases

Country/ Region	Mode of secession	Supported/ unsupported	Status of statehood
South Sudan	Self-determination/ Referendum	Supported	Recognized
Somaliland	Unilateral Declaration	Unsupported	Unrecognized
Western Sahara	Unilateral Dectlaration/ Negotiation	Unsupported	Unrecognized
Country/ Region	Mode of secession	Supported/ unsupported	Status of statehood
South Sudan	Self-determination/ Referendum	Supported	Recognized
Somaliland	Unilateral Declaration	Unsupported	Unrecognized
Western Sahara	Unilateral Declaration/ Negotiation	Unsupported	Unrecognized

Table 2: Relevance of Hypotheses to the Three Cases

Hypotheses	South Sudan	Somaliland	Western Sahara
History of conflict	Yes	No	No
Compatible norms and internationalized ethnic politics	Yes	No	No
Status of mother state in international community	Yes	No	No
Security and stability interests	Yes	No	No
Agreed framework/commitment of local population	Yes/Yes	No/Yes	Yes/Yes
Economic benefits	No	No	Yes

4.3 Comparative Method

The use of comparative method generated meaningful contrasts for my three cases, distinguishing the strong support for South Sudan's secession as explicitly demonstrated in the arguments above. But is the comparative method suitable in a social science context? Whether it is a method of difference or agreement, John Stuart Mill cautions that the comparative method is unsuitable for solving social science problems (Mill, 1872: 280). As argued by Stanley Lieberson, Mill specifically illustrates the inapplicability of the method of difference by describing differences between nations and observes the weakness of the method of agreement for typical social science questions (Lieberson, 1991: 308). With reference to my Table 2, it was difficult to get one causal variable that could explain the uniqueness of South Sudan's secession; rather, the four hypotheses (variables) stand together to explain the unique support for South Sudan's secession. Moreover, it is difficult to infer that the four hypotheses are deterministic and thus unique to the case of South Sudan, but probably the four can be showed to be identical for the South Sudan case as literature and interviews showed. However, the condition for absence of interaction effects on the variables further impedes the method. For example, in my case, a variable (hypothesis) such as the status of the mother state in the eyes of the international community has an interaction with

SUCCESSFUL AND FAILED SECESSIONS

the variable (hypothesis) of security and stability interests of the great powers, as shown in empirical literature, and it is always difficult in social science to avoid this. Therefore, the comparative method can only be meaningful when combined with other methodological tools, such as process tracing and counterfactual, but will always have limitations because our knowledge is probabilistic.

5. Conclusions

―⟨∘⟩―

THIS BOOK HAS PRESENTED a strong argument. In investigating the reasons why South Sudan's secession was strongly supported, I conceptualized the understanding of secession through the right of self-determination, using comparative politics sub-discipline and applying realist theory, an international relations sub-discipline approach to explain the power and interests of the great powers in the extension of diplomatic recognition.

The aim of this book has been to investigate the reasons that led to the great powers' support to South Sudan's secession. I examined domestic and international environment in order to represent factors and tested these as hypotheses. The domestic factors included: history of conflict; agreed framework and commitment of local population, whereas my international factors include compatible norms and internationalized ethnic politics; status of the mother state in international community; economic benefits, and security and stability interests. After testing these with the empirical literature and by conducting elite interviews and comparing them with Somaliland and Western Sahara, it became apparent that the secession of South Sudan was overwhelmingly supported because of the history of conflict as a domestic factor and the compatible norms and internationalized ethnic politics, the diminished status of Sudan in the eyes of the international community, and security and stability interests as international factors. The two hypotheses of an agreed framework and commitment of local population, and economic benefits, turned out not to be distinct for the case of South

Sudan. The former is shared by both Somaliland and Western Sahara, since they also had local people committed to their independence, and Western Sahara also has an agreed framework of self-determination like South Sudan. The economic benefits argument turned out not to be relevant to South Sudan because of the low interest shown by Western powers, particularly the U.S in its resources. This was also irrelevant to Somaliland because its former home state does not have substantial resources to attract the great powers' support. The economic benefits factor was only relevant in the case of Western Sahara because of U.S. and French interests in Morocco's resources.

Throughout my argument, the "Troika" and other Western European countries have been my focus, although the U.S. appeared as my core focus of analysis given a leading role it played in South Sudan's independence. My conceptual framework of; norms of sovereignty and realist theory has provided a useful understanding of the interests of the great powers in supporting secessions and recognition. It has been clarified that the conferment of sovereignty is hypocritical and that recognition is motivated by interests that breach the Montevideo Convention on the Rights and Duties of States. Although I do not claim to have 'proven' my comparative method, a combination of process tracing has helped in the in-depth analysis of all six hypotheses. Therefore, we can see that support to South Sudan's secession is embedded in the political realism of international politics. The valid hypotheses of the history of conflict; compatible norms and internationalized ethnic politics; the status of the mother state in the eyes of the international community, and the security and stability interests are more of concern to the great powers than to the African Union.

Although the South Sudan case appears unique in comparison with Somaliland and Western Sahara, the four distinct factors cannot be generalized to represent other successful secessions such as Eritrea and Timor-Leste. It remains the case that the unique support for South Sudan's secession is motivated by the national interests of Western great powers under the leadership of the U.S, which challenges the notion of African boundaries being sacrosanct. Since this is a new area of scholarship, which I do not claim to have exhausted, future research will be important in order to further investigate; either to confirm or refute each of my four hypotheses explaining the Western great powers' support for the birth of the state of South Sudan.

Bibliography

Alier, A (2003) 'Too Many Agreements Dishonoured: Southern Sudan', Lebanon, Ithac.

Avlon, J (2011) 'The Birth of a Nation', July 9. http://www.thedailybeast.com/articles/2011/07/09/birth-of-a-nation.html (September 1, 2012)

Bahaijoub, A (2010) 'Western Sahara Conflict: Historical and International Dimensions', London, North-South.

BG & SAIS (2009) 'Why the Maghreb matters: threats, opportunities & options for effective US Engagement in North Africa', Special report-March: 1-15.

Bridget, L (2006) 'Secession, Recognition and the International Politics of Statehood', PhD Dissertation: The Ohio State University.

Cockett, R (2010) 'Sudan, Darfur and the Future of an African State', New Haven, Yale.

Colins, T (2012) 'Russia claims US interest in S. Sudan motivated by oil', January 17. http://www.sudantribune.com/Russia-claims-US-interest-in-S,41308 (August 9, 2012).

Crawford, J (2006) 'The Creation of States in International Law', 2nd edition, London, Oxford.

Dahlitz, J (2003) 'Secession and International Law: Conflict Avoidance: Regional Appraisals', Geneva, United Nations.

Dau, I (2011) 'Free at Last: South Sudan Independence and the Role of the Church', Nairobi, Kijabe.

Deng, F (1995) 'War of Visions: Conflicts of Identities in the Sudan', Washington, Brookings.

Deng, F (2009) 'Frontiers of Unity: An Experiment in

Afro-Arab cooperation: The Ngok Dinka of Southern Sudan and the Abyei Experiment with African-Arab Cooperation', London, Kegan Paul.

Gibbs, D (1991) 'The Political Economy of Third World Intervention: Mines, Money, and U.S. Policy in the Congo Crisis', Chicago.

Halton, D (2007) 'Faith and Politics: The Rise of Religions Rights and Its Impact on American Domestic and Foreign Policy', Larkin-Stuart Lectures, March 8-9th.

Hamilton, R (2011) 'U.S. Played Key Role in Southern Sudan's Long Journey to Independence', Pulitzer Centre on Crisis reporting: 1-4.

Hertzke, A (2004) 'Freeing God's Children: The Unlikely Alliance for Global Human Rights', Annual Paul Henry Lecture, Calvin College-November 11th.

Ismael, A (2002) 'Somaliland: The Myth of Clan-Based Statehood', December 7. http://www.somaliawatch.org/archive-dec02/021207202.htm (September 1, 2012).

Jennings, Ivor (1956) 'The Approach to Self-Government', London, Cambridge.

Jensen, E (2012) 'Western Sahara: Anatomy or Stalemate?', 2nd edition, London, Lynne Rienner.

Johnson, F (2011) 'Waging Peace in Sudan: the inside Story of the Negotiations That Ended Africa's Longest Civil War', Brighton, Sussex.

Johnson, H (2012) 'British policy in Anglo-Egyptian Sudan bears some responsibility for the deep-rooted divisions between the North and South', July 2. http://blogs.lse.ac.uk/africaatlse/2012/07/02/british-policy-in-anglo-egyptian-sudan-bears-some-responsibility-for-the-deep-rooted-divisions-between-north-and-south (September 1, 2012).

Knox, C (2012) 'The Secession of South Sudan: A Case Study in African and International Recognition', Political Science Student Work. Paper 1.

Krasner, S (1999) 'Sovereignty: Organized Hypocrisy', Princeton NJ, Princeton.

Lieberson, S (1991) 'Small N's and Big Conclusions: An Examination of the Reasoning in Comparative Studies Based on a Small Number of Cases', Social Forces 70 (2): 307-320.

Lokosang. L (2010) 'South Sudan: The Case for Independence and Learning from Mistakes', U.S., Xlibris.

Mail and Guidance (2012) 'AU Supports Somali Split', February 10.www.mg.co.za/article/2006-02-10-au-supports-somali-split (August 9, 2012).

Mill, J (1872) 'System of Logic, Ratiocinative and Inductive', 8th edition, New York, Harper and Brothers.

Moore, M (2003) 'National Self-Determination and Secession', London, Oxford.

Morgenthau, H (2006) 'Politics among Nations: the struggle for power and peace', 7th edition revised by Kenneth W & David Clinton., U.S., McGraw Hill.

Osiander, A (2001) 'Sovereignty, International Relations and the Westphalian Myth', International Organization 55 (2): 251-287.

Paquin, J (2004) 'The United States, Secessionist Movements and Stability', Quebec, McGill, Montreal.

Pavkovic, A and Radan P (2007) 'Creating New States: Theory and Practice of secession', London, Ashgate.

Reynolds, P (2008) 'Somaliland: Path to Recognition', BBC News, April 25. http://news.bbc.co.uk/1/hi/world/africa/7365002.stm (August 9, 2012).

Roble, F (2007) 'Local and Global Norms: Challenges to Somaliland's Unilateral Secession', Horn of Africa Studies Vol XXV: 1-19.

Rustow, D (1970) 'Transitions to Democracy: Toward a Dynamic Model', Comparative Politics, 2(3): 337-363.

Saideman, S (1997) 'Explaining the International Relations of Secessionist conflicts: Vulnerability Versus Ethnic Ties', International Organization 51 (4): 721-753.

Siroky, D (2009) 'Secession and Survival: Nations, States and Violent conflict', PhD dissertation-Duke University.

Strang, D (1990) 'Anomaly and Commonplace in

European Political Expansion', International Organization: 45 (2)143-162.

Sudan Tribune (2012) 'Obama adds South Sudan to List of Countries Eligible to Receive US Weapons', January 7. http://www.sudantribune.com/Obama-adds-South-Sudan-to-list-of,41207 (August 9, 2012).

Woodrow, W (1918) 'Speech on the Fourteen Points', Congressional Record, 65th Congress 2nd Session: 680-681.

Field interviewees

Ambra Longatti, Deputy Head of Office-European Union, Juba, 29/06/2012.

Christopher Datta, Deputy Chief of Mission, USA Embassy, Juba, 4/07/2012.

Cirino Hiteng, Minister of Youth, Sports and Culture-GOSS, Juba, 28/06/2012.

Emmanuel LoWilla, Minister in the Office of President-GOSS, Juba, 3/07/2012.

Jok Madut, Author and Undersecretary of Ministry of

Youth, Sports and Culture-GOSS, Juba, 2/07/2012.

Michael Makuei, Minister of Parliamentary Affairs-GOSS and Negotiator on South Sudan post-referendum issues, Juba, 29/06/2012.

Appendix 1

———◦◦———

A Sample Interview Guide for South Sudanese's Elites

1. Do you think the secession of South Sudan from the North was an appropriate decision for South Sudan? If yes or no, why?

2. In your opinion, do you think South Sudan's secession was strongly supported? If yes or no? Please explain briefly.

3. Do you think history of wars and ethnic identity played a role in the support for South Sudan's secession? If yes or no, please explain.

4. Do you think the great powers' support for South Sudan's secession was motivated by campaigns for the secession option by local populations? If yes or no, why?

5. Do you think religion, for example Christianity made the great powers such as U.S. and EU support the South Sudanese secession against the North? If yes or no, why?

6. Do you think the U.S. Black caucus and evangelicals played any critical role in campaigning for the South Sudan independence? If yes or no, explain.

7. Did western civil society organizations, such as Enough Project and media fraternity, play any role in supporting South Sudanese independence? If yes or no, please explain.

8. Do you think human rights violations and abuses by Khartoum's government made the great powers support South Sudan's statehood? If yes or no, how?

9. Did the issuance of an arrest warrant to President Al-Bashir by ICC contribute to the support for South Sudan

THE BIRTH OF STATES: SUCCESSFUL AND FAILED SECESSIONS

secession by the great powers? If yes or no, please explain.

10. Do you think that the regional and the great powers' support for South Sudan secession was motivated by material resources benefit such as oil? If yes or no, why?

11. Do you think countries, such as the U.S. and Israel's support for South Sudan's independence was driven by national security interests of their countries against Khartoum? If yes or no, please explain briefly.

12. How unique is the South Sudan case for secession, given that the regional and the great powers massively support it, while they failed to support the Somaliland and Western Sahara secessions?

Appendix 2

A Sample Interview Guide for the Great Powers

1. What role did your region/country play in the Comprehensive Peace Agreement (CPA) between the North and South Sudan?

2. Did your region/country support the secession of South Sudan in any way? If yes or no, why?

3. Do you think history of wars and ethnic identity made your region/country supportive for South Sudan's secession? If yes or no, please explain.

4. Was your support encouraged by the opinion polls indicating secession as the overwhelming choice of the people of South Sudan? If yes or no, why?

5. Do you think ideology such as religion, e.g. Christianity made your region/country support the secession of South Sudan? If yes or no, why?

6. Did western civil society organizations campaigns influence the success of South Sudan's secession? If yes, who were they and why? If no, briefly explain.

7. Do you think poor governance such as human rights abuses in Darfur, by government of Sudan, made your region/country to support South Sudan's statehood? If yes or no, please explain briefly.

8. Did the issuance of an arrest warrant to President Al-Bashir by ICC make your country more supportive toward South Sudanese secession? If yes or no, please explain.

9. Was your country support for South Sudan's secession motivated by material resources benefit, such as oil? If yes

or no, briefly explain.

10. Do you think countries/organizations such, as U.S and EU, support for South Sudan secession was driven by national security interests against Northern Sudan?

11. How unique is South Sudan's secession, given that the regional and the great powers massively support it, while withholding the secessions of Somaliland and Western Sahara?

Field Interviewees

Ambra Longatti, Deputy Head of Office-European Union, Juba, 29/06/2012.

Christopher Datta, Deputy Chief of Mission, USA Embassy, Juba, 4/07/2012.

Cirino Hiteng, Minister of Youth, Sports and Culture-GOSS, Juba, 28/06/2012.

Emmanuel LoWilla, Minister in the Office of President-GOSS, Juba, 3/07/2012.

Jok Madut, Author and Undersecretary of Ministry of Youth, Sports and Culture-GOSS, Juba, 2/07/2012.

Michael Makuei, Minister of Parliamentary Affairs-GOSS and Negotiator on South Sudan post-referendum issues, Juba, 29/06/2012.

Index

Juba 19, 39-40, 59, 85-6, 93-4

Julie 6

Katanga 51

Kegan 81

Kenneth 83

Kenya 19, 57

Kenyan 53

Khartoum 30-31, 47, 58-9, 64, 66-7, 89

Kiir 21

Kijabe 80

Knox, C. 30, 82

Kong 11

Koran 31

Kordofan 58

Krasner, S. 10-13, 82

Laayoune 24

Latin 26

Lebanon 79

Libya 57

Lieberson, S. 72, 83

Logic 83

Lokosang 83

London 11, 79-84

Longatti 85, 93

Lynne 82

Lzik 41

Machakos 35

Machar 21

Madut 53, 85, 94

Maghreb 24, 49, 55, 61-2, 79

Mahidiya 29

Makuei 38, 86, 94

Malawi 57

Malaysia 53, 69

Mauritania 25, 34

Mayardit 21

Mediterranean 61

Michael 38, 45, 65, 86, 94

Mogadishu 54, 66

Mohammed 32

Montevideo 15-16, 77

Montreal 84

Moore, M. 83

Morgenthau, H. 14, 83

Moroccan 25-27, 37, 41

Morocco 24-28, 34, 48-9, 54-5, 61, 67-9

Muslim 27, 46

Muslims 43, 65